THE
Archive Photographs
SERIES

GARSTON

The Old Cottage. We start and finish this book with the picture of the Old Cottage which stood at the heart of the village of Garston, and tell the story in between.

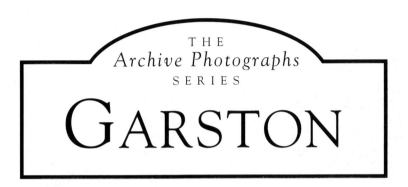

THE
Archive Photographs
SERIES

GARSTON

Compiled by
Margaret and Bernard Brett
and the
Garston and District Historical Society

CHALFORD

First published 1996
Copyright © Margaret and Bernard Brett and the
Garston and District Historical Society, 1996

The Chalford Publishing Company
St Mary's Mill, Chalford,
Stroud, Gloucestershire, GL6 8NX

ISBN 0 7524 0676 0

Typesetting and origination by
The Chalford Publishing Company
Printed in Great Britain by
Redwood Books, Trowbridge

The Parish Church and the gas holder, a familiar sky line.

Contents

The Garston Crest.

Acknowledgements

The editorial panel: Margaret and Bernard Brett, Rebecca Black, Roy Forshaw, Bill Hitchen, Ann Holland, Roy Lovering, Pam Otten, Margaret Purcell, Fred Sykes, Jim Williams.

Thanks also to those who, in addition to the above, gave information, lent photographs or gave permission for photographs to be used. These include: Peter Turner, Doris Ball, Jean Leadbetter, Dorothy Griffiths, Richard Stansfield, Muriel Lloyd, Dorothy Pyle, Phil Mobbs, Nancy Jackson, Eileen Crook, Barbara Price, Anesta Jeffrey, Jim McLoughlan, Mr Evans, Bill Jones, Tom King, Pam Fleetwood, Barbara Blanthorn, Mrs Kay, John Derbyshire, Bob and Beattie Atherton, Mrs Mayers, Kay Gibbard, Mrs Slack, Mrs Pugh, Les Denton, Dave Crumpton, Ken Rawlinson, Josie Kerbey, Shirley Smith, Geoff Mason, Graham Earle, Tom Owen, Tom Mather, Brian Taylor, A. Powney (Holy Trinity School), Mrs Lester (Garston C of E School), and the residents of Garston who gave information during the Garston Carnival of 1996. Also John Ryan, Aerofilms Limited and John Mills Photography for permission to use their photographs and the The Old Bank Photo Copying Service, for their help and patience.

Throughout the publication much information has been gleaned from *The Story of Garston and its Church*, by the late Revd J.M. Swift MA (Hons, Cantab.), Vicar of Garston from 1929 to 1945.

The work and research involved in completing this book has revealed even further the large amount of historic material in the hands of individuals and organisations – Garston and District Historical Society is concerned to continue to collect this material for the benefit of future generations. Anyone able to contribute more information, loan, or give items, is asked to contact the society through Margaret and Bernard Brett – 0151 427 2544.

Introduction

Garston today appears to the passer-by as a struggling suburb of the great City of Liverpool. The opening of Garston Way, the by-pass, has removed commuter traffic from a route through 'the village' so that Garston is hardly even seen by many people – unless, that is, the speedy driver notices for the first time the docks, the gas works and the Parish Church, these now being more easily visible. Older inhabitants of Garston will speak of the days when St Marys Road was a thriving, densely crowded High Street and 'Under the Bridge' was characterised by a large population with plenty of work available in well known and proud factories. The centre of Garston is still 'the village'.

During the period between the the First and Second World Wars Garston peaked in its industrial and dock-trade development and indeed, during the Second World War, as an adjunct to the great Port and City of Liverpool, doubtless played its part in the economic and military survival of the nation. Garston then shared the economic decline and the transfer of trading which has affected Liverpool and Merseyside during the last half century.

The publication of this book – not a history of Garston as such, but a collection of 'life and times' photographs – happens to coincide with the Speke/Garston Partnership, whereby Government and European money to the tune of many millions is to be spent on attracting and developing new industries and in improving the social, environmental, shopping and leisure facilities to enhance the quality of life for the population of this once proud town.

The development of Garston from agricultural village to small industrial town and port is a dramatic story too often ignored when the stories of the other, more salubrious villages of Liverpool are told. The existence of Garston as a settlement undoubtedly owes its origins to the Garston River, a powerful brook having its source in the Allerton and Mossley Hill areas and which provided power for water mills, for irrigation and fresh water fishing. Here also was land, timber, clay and stone and water transport possibilities alongside road access to and from Speke and beyond, as well as through Toxteth Park to the City of Liverpool.

In 1264 one Adam de Gerston, then Lord of the Manor, gave his tanning and fulling mill and associated land and water rights to the monks of Stanlawe, near Bromborough on the Wirral. The monks subsequently moved to Whalley but maintained their interest in the area. Garston Hall and Aigburth Hall with its granary, continued to be used for supplies of fish, grain and cloth no doubt, and both halls were used as places of worship.

In those days and until the middle of the nineteenth century, Garston would have still presented a delightful village and country scene. Its strong brook would be flowing where, in evidence, is the slight hollow in Horrocks Avenue, then along by the site of what is now the swimming baths, turning sharply towards the Mersey parallel to Church Road in order to power Adam de Gerston's Mill (beneath and behind the former Blackburne Arms) and then flowing out to where Stalbridge Dock is now located. Below Adam's Mill, the brook flowed through a wooded gorge affording a delightful walk on a sunny evening and known as the Dale or Dingle. The first industry, apart from those already mentioned, was the salt works of 1790, signalling the dramatic changes which were soon to follow when this green field sight was identified by industrial developers as an area ripe for development, especially because of its river position.

In a very short period large and small industries were attracted to the farm fields and the dock potential: ship building, sugar works, vitriol works, copper works, the tannery, the largest bobbin and shuttle works in the world, iron and steel works, bottle works, metallurgical works, the gas works and later the match factory, while on the docks there developed the banana trade and the import and export of dozens of different kinds of manufactured goods and raw materials, resulting from world-wide and coastal trade links.

Many of the pictures in this book are about the lives and activities of those who lived and worked in Garston. Because of the expanding industries and trade the indigenous population was added to by people from nearby areas as well as from Wales, inland Lancashire and Cheshire. Shops, societies, clubs, churches and schools were established in addition to the leisure and servicing facilities needed by a thriving community. Although changing circumstances have taken many people away and others have come to live in the area, there remains a core of families representing several generations of Garstonians, with the history of Garston built into their memories and recorded in the photographs which are now reproduced.

Bernard Brett, August 1996

An aerial view of the docks and industry.

One

Beginnings

An early drawing of the village scene, looking up Chapel Road, leading to Woolton Road, from Church Road. The cottage to the right was in existence until around the mid 1920s. Garston Hall occupies a prominent position and below it, the Garston Village Cross, later to be moved when Speke Road, coming in from the right, was to be continued as St Marys Road. The Garston river flows from the pool in front of the cottage and round towards us to feed the dam for the mill dating back to Adam de Gerston. The old National School is opposite the Hall, in the area known as Kettle Nook. Beyond this, sometime later, the Sir Alfred Lewis Jones Memorial Hospital was built on the site of what was once a brickfield.

Garston Hall, formerly a grange of Stanlawe Abbey. This Hall, which once contained a Roman Catholic Chapel, later became a farmhouse and was eventually demolished.

The old Village Cross. Now in the grounds of St Francis of Assisi Church, Earp Street, this cross originally stood in the centre of the village. It was lost for a time then re-sited with an iron cross superimposed outside the Heald Chapel in Chapel Road. The grooves are thought to be sockets for punishment stocks.

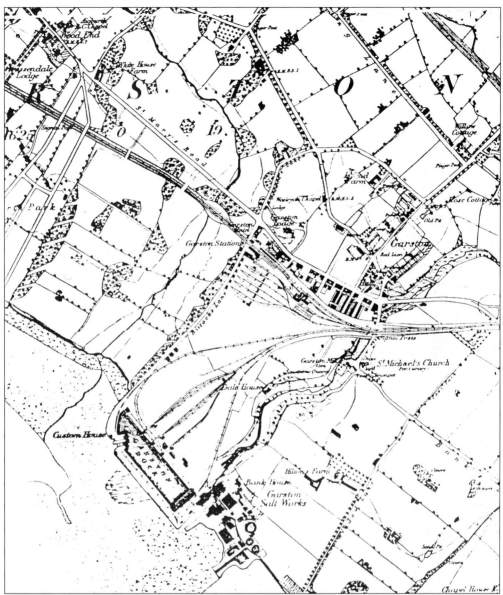

The map shows the village of Garston around 1850. The St Helen's Canal and Railway Company have built the New Dock alongside the salt works of 1790. The Garston River is now crossed by the railway line, Speke Road has been continued as St Marys Road and the Garston River running through The Willows, formerly a dam, has gone underground to reappear as the dam pool for Adam's Mill, subsequently forming the picturesque Dale or Dingle running down to the River Mersey. Early churches, hotels, stations, houses, cottages and farms are now in evidence. The mediaeval village is becoming an industrial town and port.

From the country village grew the town. This view shows St Marys Road, Speke Road, Church Road and Chapel Road corner at the turn of the century. The river flowed culverted beneath the road. The Mona Castle pub on the right was partly built on the rocky promontory where, further back, once stood Garston Hall.

The docks meanwhile, had developed with the addition of the North Dock (1864) and the Stalbridge Dock (1903), complementing and serving the industrial area.

Stanlawe Grange was the converted granary in Aigburth Hall Avenue, said to be one of the oldest buildings in Liverpool. It was used by the monks of Stanlawe and continued to be used by them when they moved their Abbey from the Wirral to Whalley in Lancashire.

The original boundary of the township of Garston extended northwards to Aigburth Vale and in the other direction to the boundary with Speke, which was close by Burnsall Street. The horse drawn omnibus took passengers travelling from Liverpool on the electric tram, which terminated at Aigburth Vale, on to Garston.

Speke Hall. The manor of Garston was at one time held by Helena, wife of Robert de Blackburne. Then, until 1736, it was held by the Norris family of Speke Hall. The Norrises gave much support to the church in Garston and Miss Adelaide Watt, a later owner of Speke Hall, was also a substantial benefactress of the Parish Church as well as supporting other Garston developments.

Two

Early Days

Mr and Mrs Entwistle, of Island Road, sitting just inside the gates of the Whitehedge Road and Brodie Avenue corner of the Garston Recreational Ground. The Recreational Ground was opened in 1902 and to take a walk to the furthest end from Garston, as this couple did, was to go into the countryside; there was no Brodie Avenue, nor were there any houses in that part of Whitehedge Road at that time. The iron railings were removed for armaments manufacture during the Second World War.

A view of Garston Docks from Cressington Promenade. Notice the sailing ships, Mersey Flats (sailing barges), and a steam ship.

The corner of Aigburth Road and Grassendale Road. Woodend Farm (Kettlewells, later Dugdales) is on the right. St Austin's church gateway is on the left, St Mary's Church spire is hidden by trees, but the Church Hall is just visible in the distance. In recent years the farm site has become a petrol station.

White House Farm (Akriggs), at the corner of Whitehedge Road and St Marys Road, (opposite St Mary's church). The barn on the corner has already gone and the house was demolished in 1931.

Garston Old Road, looking towards St Mary's Church, taken from a point near to the present row of shops. St Marys Terrace, only just visible through trees on the right, was built in 1852. The building of the houses between Duncombe Road North and St Marys Road began in 1925.

Garston Old Mill is one of the oldest landmarks in Garston. The original mill on this site was referred to as Adam de Gerstan's Mill of 1264 and was a fulling mill powered by the river which flowed out to the Mersey. Later it was a corn and spice mill owned by James Wood and later still, among its many uses, it was Massey's scrap yard. In the 1930s it was used as a boys club and was visited by Edward, Prince of Wales.

Church Road around the turn of the century. Passers by watch the goats being driven home. The refuse destructor chimney can be seen behind the signal box and the hospital incinerator chimney between the signals.

Old cottages at the corner of Church Road and Speke Road. The entrance to Mason's forge can be seen on the right. It is said that the structure in front was used as a stall for selling beverages by two ladies who also had interests in the Cocoa Rooms near by. One of the last inhabitants was Paddy Flynn, a seller of vegetables and quite a well known local character. The cottages were demolished in the mid 1920s. At the suggestion of the Garston and District Historical Society, the Leading Light, an artefact rescued from loss during developments on the docks, now stands in its place.

An artist's impression of the village corner; the cottages in the previous picture have been replaced by the Irwin's shop building, set a little farther back. The shops on the right were demolished some years ago and the buildings on the left, including Inghams the cobblers, have also gone.

Kettle Nook. This was an area near where the hospital gates now stand. It consisted of at least three blocks of houses: Rose Mount, Mount Pleasant and Rimmer's Terrace. At one time the tenants of the latter were, the Stowes, Westwoods, Pownalls and Ashcrofts and the last tenants of Mount Pleasant, around the mid 1930s, were the Davies, Jones and Davies families. It has been suggested that the name Kettle Nook was given to it because of the water pump, where people filled their kettles. The square building on the left was the National School, built in 1716. When the school moved to a new site the ground floor of the old building then became the Cocoa Rooms and the upper floor was used as a Sunday School. The building was demolished around the time of the First World War, during the building of the hospital.

The old Lock-up prison, on the corner of Rimmer's Terrace, which is shown on a 1717 map. The site became the mortuary, which has also gone.

Two cottages, at the turn of the century, near the railway end of what would later become Tudwall Street. The lady on the right is thought to be 'Granny Ireland', since it is known that she lived there and was allowed to graze her hens on the Spion Cop at the rear. It is also known that she washed the church choir surplices; are those the necessary utensils on the right?

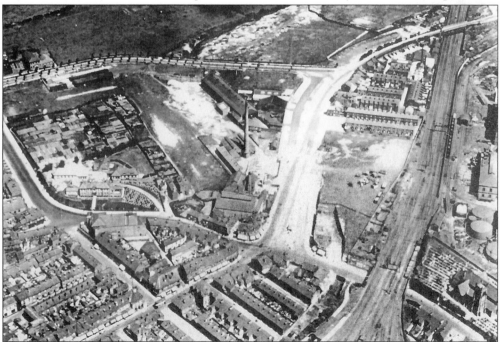

On this aerial photograph can be seen a number of the sites referred to in the last few pictures. Note also the travelling fair on the Spion Cop, the new (white) roofs of the recently built wash house and new ward added to the hospital. Horrocks Avenue has not yet been constructed, nor Conder Close; the market can be clearly seen near the top left of the picture. Also at the top right, Bridge Cottages are visible.

Brunswick Street: a row of cottages built by the owners of the copper works for their workers. Since many of these came from Wales, they were sometimes called the Welsh Cottages. The manager's house, Bankfield House, would be just off the picture to the right. They were also known as the 'back to front houses' because they have no road access at the fronts, only to their back gates. It is said that Miss Watt, of Speke Hall, insisted they be built in this way so that the tenants could look over green fields to the Hall, or was it so that she did not have to look at their washing on the line? This latter story has become part of the Garston folklore.

A cottage in Banks Road occupied by the Clifford family and, at one time, by Mr Christian the chimney sweep.

Bridge Cottages were situated on the Garston side of the railway by the Speke Road bridge. They were built long before the railway, alongside the road called Green Lane or Green Gate Lane. There were six cottages, two of which were back to back with the centre ones. Living there in 1907 were, at No.1, Mrs Mary Kelly, a laundress, at No.3, Thomas Reynolds, at No. 5, James Flemming, at No.7, William Burgess, at No.9, Robert Nugent and at No.11, Elizabeth Ireland. In later years the Ward family lived at No. 5 and the Wykes also lived in one of the buildings. The last tenant is thought to have been Mr Rigby. The cottages were demolished for the widening of the road in 1936.

Cabbage Harvest. This fascinating photograph was taken in Speke Road. Chapel Farm farmhouse is on the left. In the picture from left to right are: Bert Rigby, Jim Smith, Mr Rigby, (farmer), Miss Dickinson (in First World War Land Army uniform), Mrs Dickinson and Mrs Wyke.

Chapel Farm farmhouse. This was often referred to as 'the house with ten windows'. In 1907 it was lived in by Mrs Hitchmough, however the last tenant was Mr John Rigby. He and his family left in 1936 and the Liverpool Corporation immediately demolished the house to complete the dual carriageway construction of the road.

Beech House. In 1907 Police Constable John Deering lived in the house and after him, Mr Shone and his family lived there. The site was later occupied by what became the New Cavalier pub and eating place. More recently the building has been converted for motor trade use.

Speke Road in 1928, before alterations to the bridge and road, looking towards Speke. On the left can be seen Chapel Farm and behind the signals, Beech House. Vineyard Street and Meredith Street are just visible beyond these. To the right of the road can be seen the Bryant and May match works and the recently built (1926) workers' houses.

Speke Road Gardens' Tenements were built in 1932 on the site that had at one time been Cowen's nursery garden and before that, Mr Meredith's vineyards. His grapes were highly thought of and won many awards. They were enjoyed by Queen Victoria and the Pope: in 1869 a letter was sent in appreciation from his Eminence. The quality of the grapes was well known throughout Europe as Mr Meredith supplied, among others, Emperor Napoleon III and the King of Prussia. Vineyard Street and Meredith Street are obviously named after this illustrious gentleman.

The same site as above but viewed here after the demolition of the Tenements in 1983, with the construction of new housing just beginning. Vineyard Street and Meredith Street are clearly visible. What changes the people living in these streets have seen over the last sixty years!

26

Three
Docks and Industry

A postcard version of a national advertising poster shows the importance given to Garston. The London Midland and Scottish Railway took over the port in 1921. Previously, the London and North Western Railway had owned the port, having taken over from the St Helen's Coal and Railway Company which had built the first enclosed dock, the Old Dock, in about 1850. After the LMS, British Rail ran the dock, then the British Transport Commission until Associated British Ports took over.

Garston Old Dock. This busy scene shows the coal tipping equipment (right) which discharged coal direct from railway wagons into the holds of the ships. The dock was built to take coal for domestic use to Northern Ireland and also to supply the growing number of steam ships using the Port of Liverpool. Coal was also used locally and transported via coastal vessels for industrial and domestic purposes to other parts of the country.

Alongside coal a wide range of other products and materials were exported and imported. Eventually this included timber, minerals, fruit, iron and steel, fuel oil, molasses and china clay. Here in the North Dock, built in 1867, are sailing ships and barrels waiting to be loaded. Coal tipping equipment is now seen on the left of the photograph.

Garston Dock office staff, *c.* 1920.

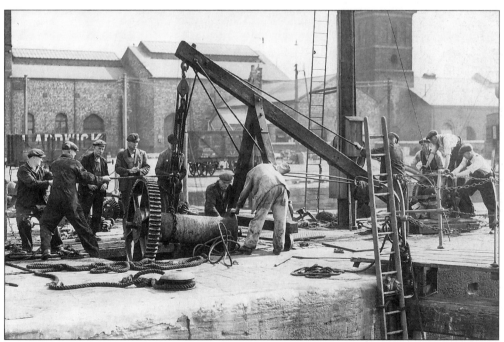

All hands to the crane as dock workers attend to the maintenance of one of the hydraulic powered capstans near the North Dock in a scene around 1940. The pump house is seen in the background.

The third and largest main dock to be built, in 1909, was the Stalbridge Dock, (Lord Stalbridge was the Chairman of the Railway Company). To the right can be seen the gas works and below this the housing area and the Garston Tannery. In the foreground on the right is the special Fyffes Banana Warehouse. Fyffes originally had fifty-two special ships, half of which were lost during the war. Having once dealt with over 50 per cent of United Kingdom imports via Garston, the banana trade moved to Southampton in the 1960s.

The Leading Light. This once stood at the entrance of one of the docks to lead vessels safely through the gates. When alterations were made so that it was no longer required, it was rescued and placed on the site of the Old Cottage in the centre of the village, as a symbol of Garston Port history. This operation was arranged by the then Merseyside County Council, at the request of the Garston Community Council and in consultation with the Garston and District Historical Society.

Alongside the docks there developed substantial industries, serviced by the docks and railways. Top left can be seen the Graving Dock, the J.M. Mills distillery, Garston Tanning Company and below this, a small part of the Francis Morton Company Ltd iron and steel works. Middle left is the Wilson Brothers Bobbin Company Ltd.

The Graving Dock, now filled in, and the J.M. Mills distillery, now demolished.

Messrs Wilson Brothers Bobbin Works Ltd established an office in 1902 and over a period of years moved their works from Cornholme near Todmordon, to Garston. They became the largest bobbin and shuttle manufacturers in the world, with a fleet of five schooners bringing rare woods from many countries and exporting products likewise. They employed 1,400 workers producing a million bobbins a week.

Bobbin workers outside the main factory gate in Blackburne Street.

A group of women workers at the bobbin works with medical staff. Miss Hepple, the Matron is centre back. Also in the picture are two of the three Elbert sisters: Katie (second left) and Nellie (right) both kneeling. They and their sister Maggie (not in picture), married three Jackson brothers: Jim, Robert and William.

Office staff at the bobbin works.

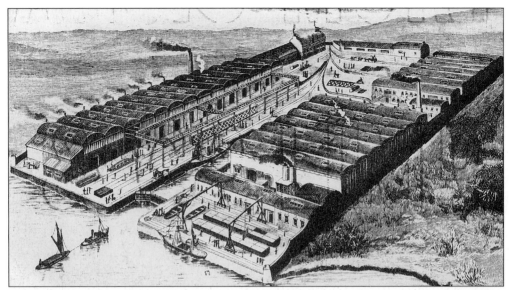

From 1880 Francis Morton & Company Ltd became a very large concern, supplying, among other notable projects, iron work for the Liverpool Overhead Railway, Clarence Dock Power Station and Everton Football Ground. They also produced many bridges and prefabricated iron railway stations, barracks, schools and churches which were exported all over the world.

Francis Morton Ironworks' employees in front of a steam crane, before 1960.

Workers at the Garston Tannery, King Street, in 1914. The tannery is now the only industry to have survived from the past. The site is a stone's throw from where, in 1264, Adam de Gerstan had his mill which was used for tanning amongst other things. In 1899, Messrs John, Joseph, and Francis Boston moved their family business from the north end of Liverpool to its present site as they needed to expand. At one time numbered among the largest tanneries in the country, this firm still continues with a family member, Mr Nicholas Boston, at the helm.

As part of a rationalisation process, obsolete parts of the tannery plant have been removed. The boiler chimney was demolished in the late 1980s by Fred Dibnah. (Photograph courtesy of the *Liverpool Daily Post and Echo*).

Early brick workers in Garston. Bricks were produced in various places: on the hospital site, near the Blackburne Arms and alongside the gasworks. The Tushingham firm subsequently moved to Huyton and then Whiston. Many houses and other buildings in Garston were built of local Tushingham brick. The Tushingham family were prominent in Garston, owning public houses and shops.

One of Tushingham's steam lorries.

King Street. In the background is one of the largest gas holders in the country. This was named Ariel after the airy spirit in Shakespeare's *The Tempest*, who said to Prospero, 'I will divide and burn in many places'.

Rawlinson Sawmill employees in 1890 at the Wellington Street works. The works burned down (the site was later used for the building of the Technical School) and the business moved temporarily to what later became Mapleton's Nut and Health Foods factory, They then moved nearer to the docks. The firm supplied the woodwork for local buildings and they exported to many parts of the world. Mr F.J. Rawlinson was one of the first members for Garston on the Liverpool City Council and played an influential part in the development of the area.

Bryant and May Ltd match manufacturers was established in 1922, and by the 1980s the Garston works became first the major producer and then, the only producer of wooden matches in the United Kingdom. The firm was noted for its employment of many local people of several generations from one family and for the welfare services provided for its employees. Many famous match names such as Pilot, Swan Vesta and England's Glory were produced in Garston. The factory closed down in 1995, a sad day for many people.

Bryant and May Ltd mens' outing in the late 1950s.

Four

Transport

Not everyone in Garston had to rely on public transport. The affluent side of the town is depicted here with John Alexander Brodie and his chauffeur. The number plate is K8; does this mean he was the eighth person in Liverpool to register the ownership of a car? Mr Brodie lived at one time in Aigburth Hall, (Aigburth Hall Avenue). He was Liverpool's City Engineer from 1898-1925 and introduced central reservations for tramcars; he also, in 1901, patented the idea of prefabricated houses from reinforced concrete. He originally suggested the scheme for Otterspool Promenade in 1919 which was approved by the City Council in 1928. However it was not until after his death that the work was completed following the Second World War and the Promanade was officially opened in 1950. His other little known claim to fame is that he invented the football goal net in 1891. Brodie Avenue is named in honour of him.

The first tram in Garston. The first electric tram service came to Garston on 28 August 1902, running between Garston and Seaforth. This open top tram, reported to be the very first in service, is negotiating the Church Road cross roads as it runs from St Marys Road to Speke Road on its way from Liverpool.

The Boulevard, Grassendale. In an almost country setting this tram is waiting, possibly in the passing loop on Aigburth Road, by the 'T' junction of Mayfield Road. The loop allowed trams on the predominantly single line track to pass in opposite directions. Just visible on the very left of the picture is the wall of the Aigburth Hotel, demolished during the widening of Aigburth Road in 1965.

Horrocks Avenue. The No.33 tram is seen on the rise of Horrocks Avenue before turning into the tram sheds on Speke Road. The dip in the road was the site of The Willows which contained the stream from Woolton which flowed into the Garston Dam.

The Last Tram. The last tram in Garston ran in June 1953 and this crowd gave their farewells to driver Trembath and conductor Hodgson. Liverpool continued with trams for a further four years until September 1957 when the last tram ran between Pier Head and Edge Lane works.

Garston Station booking office. The original Garston Station booking office on Woolton Road was demolished between 1974 and 1978 as part of station improvements in readiness for the commencement of Merseyrail.

An early photograph of Garston Station with a narrower Woolton Road. The roadway in far from perfect condition was not the only problem. In 1881 asphalt macadam was laid on part of the carriage way tp provide a more easily cleaned surface to prevent the offensive smell of the horse manure left by the cab horses which stood outside the station.

The last train to leave Garston Station was a diesel multiple unit driven by Kenny Geddis in 1974. The line was reopened for electric trains in 1978, administered by Merseyrail.

The train leaving Church Road Station in 1905, crossing the first railway bridge over Church Road on its way towards Speke. This sandstone bridge was later replaced with an iron girder bridge as the expansion of the dock railway system took place. The view can be compared today by standing on the steps leading to the Garston Parish Church churchyard.

Church Road Station, owned by the London and North Western Railway Company, served the Garston village and 'Under the Bridge' communities. At the end of the station can be seen Garston gasworks in its Town Gas production days.

Dock Road Station. This station, shown in 1939, was a few hundred yards down the line from Church Road station and served the dock area. This photograph is looking towards the level crossing gates on Dock Road. It is said that the passenger service failed due to the competition from the trams running along St Marys Road.

This stretch of line linked Dock Road Station, behind the photographer, with Church Road Station in the distance. To the right is the siding to the docks engine sheds while the wagons in the siding to the left were for a private yard at the end of Mercer Street. Garston Way, the by-pass, has replaced the railway track.

Left: Some of the Garston Dock railway staff in 1938. Right: The committee of the London and North Western Railway Institute (Burnsall Street) in 1920. In the centre wearing the grey suit is Arthur Hughes, chairman from 1915-1950. On the far right is Robert Watling who was secretary and treasurer until 1950. He became dock manager after the Second World War.

Speke Airport, Liverpool. The first aeroplanes landed in Speke in the summer of 1930. Chapel House farmhouse was used as a control tower and for passenger facilities, while the farmyard was roofed over to provide a hangar. There was an official opening in July 1933 in the form of a Grand Air Display, watched by at least 50,000 people.

The new control tower of the Terminal Building was opened in June 1937 by Lord Derby. Many will remember viewing the aircraft movements from the public observation balcony.

Five

Life and Times

Many people in Garston claim their ancestry back to the lady on the right of this picture, 'Granny Ireland', Elizabeth Ireland who died in 1915. She was also known as the wise woman of Garston and it was said at her death that she had helped to bring over 2,000 babies into the world. The *Church Magazine* at that time recorded that she left 77 living descendants to mourn her loss, 6 children, 22 grandchildren, 35 great-grandchildren and one great-great-grandchild. She was 91 years of age at the time of her death, and lived at No.14 Gilbert Street. Also in the picture is thought to be James Wood (not to be confused with James Wood, proprietor of the Wellington Hotel) and some of his family. The early Wood, Woods and Ireland families left many descendants who sometimes inter-married: very confusing for local family historians.

Heald Street. The police station and some of its 'bobbies' together with the fire engine are on the left. The Welsh Methodist Chapel is on the right, a building used for many commercial ventures in more recent years.

Officers from Heald Street Police Station with their barrel organ, about to set off on a charity money raising effort for the Police Orphanage in Woolton.

The Soup Kitchen. As far back as 1878 an organisation was formed to give relief in kind to those workers, particularly the brickworkers, who had been put out of work because of the extreme frosts. It is said that the River Mersey froze over and you could walk across. The fund was again used in 1884 and 1885. A lady living today can remember being sent to the Reading Room in the 1920s to get a jug full of pea soup and later, scouse (stew) and bread. This was possibly during the General Strike (1926); another such centre was the Bethel Chapel in Canterbury Street, where it is thought this photograph was taken.

Garston Laundry, at one time called Tranters. It started in Granville Road and later moved to Mercer Street. Rose Jackson, a long term employee, also taught the piano to many Garston children. Her father, Detective Jackson, was the first detective to be based at Garston Police Station.

Captain E.W. Turner first visited Garston in 1866 when his ship docked in the port. He was to visit many times over the next few years and always found a welcome, particularly at the Parish Church. In 1883 he decided to retire from the sea and set up as a ship's broker in Garston. From then until his death in 1936 he worked for the town and its people. He was one of the first representatives for Garston on the Liverpool City Council, when Garston was first incorporated into Liverpool, in 1902, and was instrumental in bringing about many improvements to the area. At the age of 87 he is seen here, in the driving seat, in the early 1930s, beginning a tour of the Garston Ward on the day of a by-election. He is accompanied by Mr John Case, who also served on the Council.

Voting day in the 1940s, outside the Victoria Hall in Heald Street. Mr Pyle holding the reins and Mr Kehoe, it is thought, being greeted by Mr Clarke, the prospective City Councillor.

The Garston bell ringer Samuel Gough, born in 1822, came to Garston in 1848. He missed the bells from his country village so when a new church was built in Grassendale, in 1852, he offered to become a bell ringer. However when in 1876, the new (third) Parish Church was built in Garston, Mr Gough saw that there was room for eight bells in the tower. He was instrumental in persuading Miss Lightbody, a local benefactress, to donate her money to the bells rather than to a stained glass window. In later years Mr Gough offered to provide a clock, if the parishioners would complete the tower. Eventually he gave the three faces of the clock in memory of his wife, son and sister. The picture shows Mr Gough and his family. His daughter-in-law, seated on the right, became a JP and lived to be 100 years old.

The first Garston Bell Ringers taking a break! Standing on the right is James Wood; he came to live at the Wellington Hotel in 1853 where he was the proprietor for forty years. He was an agent for Greenalls Brewery, a farmer with eighty acres of land and at one time he owned the corn and spice mill at the junction of King Street and Church Road. He was an active member of the community and served as a church warden at St Michael's Church at one period. He died in 1901; Wood Street and James Street are named after him.

The Fever Hospital (1884-1902) on the site of the present Garston Hospital. Soiled surgical dressings were sent to be destroyed in the incinerator near the railway bridge in Church Road, behind the old cottages.

The original Garston Accident Hospital on the corner of Granville Road and Chapel Road. Negotiations were started in April 1880 with the owner of the house and shop, Mr William Standing, to rent the premises. Eventually agreeable terms were reached and the necessary alterations made at a cost of £125. The hospital was opened in 1882; it had six beds and dealt for some years with the increasing number of accidents that occurred due to the growth of the docks and industry.

Sir Alfred Lewis Jones, a shipping magnate with Elder and Fyffes, who introduced bananas to the North of England. To avoid his ships coming back from East Africa unladen, he sent men with handcarts loaded with bananas to give away and hence popularised this strange fruit. Sir Alfred lived at Oaklands, Aigburth Road. In December 1909 he became ill and in the absence of his own doctor a Dr Hurter was called in. Sir Alfred commented on the efficiency of the nurses who had attended him and the doctor took the opportunity of telling Sir Alfred of the hospital they were hoping to build in Garston. Sir Alfred showed interest in the scheme and said if plans were presented to him he would be pleased to help towards its fulfilment; sadly he died later that day. Fortunately his sister had heard the conversation and on the settlement of the estate, £10,000 was endowed towards the building of the hospital, on condition it be called the Sir Alfred Jones Memorial Hospital.

This picture shows the hospital and the now cleared site where once stood Kettle Nook and Ingham's shoe shop, on the right. On the left is the site of the demolished Mona Castle public house and shops, which in even earlier times had been the site of the Garston Hall.

The Reading Room and Lecture Hall: one of Garston's most historic buildings which was opened in 1861 through the exertions of a local benefactor Hugh Gaskill Sutton, together with public subscriptions, for the working men of Garston. It was used by the Congregational, Presbyterian, and Baptist Churches for worship before they built their own churches and also by the Parish Church for Bible classes. The Reading Room had many other uses over the years: silent films, boys' boxing club and local council office. Notably the building was used for the preliminary hearing in the controversial murder trial of Florence Maybrick – the presentation of evidence about the arsenic she allegedly used to kill her husband James Maybrick. At the subsequent Crown Court trial she was found guilty and sentenced to death. After fourteen years in prison, because of a change in law, she was released. After becoming almost derelict the Reading Room has been restored and developed as a Community Activities Centre by the Garston and District Community Council.

Garston Technical School. Situated opposite the Reading Room, this building was erected in 1894 on the site which had been Rawlinson's Sawmill, a corner of which is just visible on the left of the previous picture. The Technical School later became annexed to the Toxteth Technical College. The building is now a multi-service centre run by the local authority.

Six

School Days

The first school to be built in Garston was a cottage which was eventually called the National School, situated in what became known as Kettle Nook. It was built around 1716 and in this school thousands of Garstonians received their early education. Many who became prominent in the life of Garston and the surrounding areas were educated in the Old School. The log books only date back to 1862, when it was recorded that there were 129 pupils on the roll, with a head teacher and two pupil teachers. Other entries state, 6 November 1862, 'many country boys were absent through rain' and on the 26 November in the same year, 'many boys were late in the morning through sliding'. Earlier that year an extra afternoon holiday had been given on 31 August so that all could go and watch 'the first ship to be launched in Garston'. After serving the children for 150 years, the Old School was found to be inadequate and plans were made for a new school to be built nearer to the Parish Church 'Under the Bridge', which opened on Monday 30 July 1866. The number of pupils attending grew rapidly and within four years the building had to be extended; it could then accommodate 700 children. It is recorded that the other schools in the area at that time were, 'a Roman Catholic School at Grassendale, with an average attendance of 110 and, in contemplation, a Wesleyan School in Woodger Street to hold 150 scholars'. In the picture can be seen a class of younger children at Garston Church of England School, as the National School became known in 1907, proudly holding up their work. Note the teacher standing at the back, wearing cap and gown.

Teachers at Garston National School. Seated in the centre is Mr Robert Wright, the headmaster from 1878 to 1913. Although strict with both his staff and his pupils he was affectionately known as 'Cocky Wright' and it was not unusual to see him visiting the homes of absent pupils during the evening or even in his lunch time. After thirty-five years service he retired to live in Southport and subsequently took an active part in municipal affairs, becoming at one stage the mayor of the borough. He died in 1928.

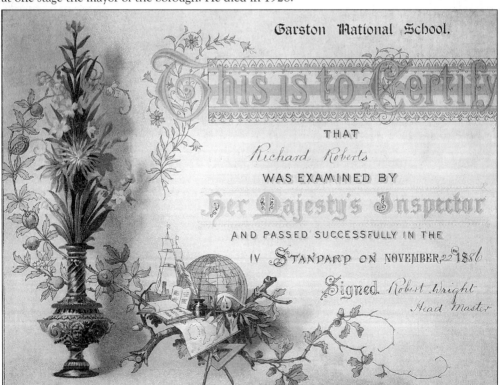

Garston National School.

This is to Certify

THAT

Richard Roberts

WAS EXAMINED BY

Her Majesty's Inspector

AND PASSED SUCCESSFULLY IN THE

IV Standard on November 22 1886

Signed Robert Wright
Head Master

Pupils and teachers of Garston Church of England School on an outing to the Houses of Parliament in 1936, where they had tea on the balcony with the MP for Garston, Mr G. Shaw. Seated in the centre are, Miss Goldstone, headmistress, Mr G. Shaw MP and Mr Oscar Brewer, headmaster. Also included among the children are Dorothy Pyle, Florence Tapp, Dorothy Wood, Vere Atkin, Ivy Southall, Peggy Ashcroft, Gertrude Williams, Thelma Pierce, Peggy Swift, Marjorie Mason, Joan Stafford, Muriel Dobson, Lucy Schwabb, Ada Southern, Florence Yates and two Dorothy Irelands. The only boy identified to us was Bobby Parkes.

Opposite: This certificate, awarded to Richard Roberts following a visit from the School Inspector in 1886, is signed by Robert Wright.

The Garston C of E School, having been on its School Street site for 100 years – in 1924 it had 1,007 children and 24 teachers – moved in 1964, in grand procession to its new building in Horrocks Avenue. Miss Radcliffe, a well known Garston figure, is in the centre of the picture, following the Vicar, Revd E.H. Isaac. Also in the group are Mr Hughes, the church warden and Mr Eaton, at one time the caretaker of the school.

The new school was officially opened on 23 June 1964 by the Bishop of London, Bishop Robert Stopford. He himself was born in Garston and educated at the Old School, where his grandfather, Mr Robert Wright, was headmaster.

St Austin's Roman Catholic School. Built in 1860, this provided for the needs of Roman Catholic children in the area until the school moved into new premises in Riverbank Road. The building then became Challoner Hall Catholic Social Club, named after the Challoner family who many years ago had great influence in the establishment of the church and school.

La Sagesse Convent School opened in the house called Holmleigh in 1910 by the Sisters of Wisdom. At that time it had ten pupils but it grew to be a large grammar school for girls. It closed in 1983 with the reorganisation of Roman Catholic education in Liverpool. Here we see teachers and pupils enjoying some time on the croquet lawn, upon which a modern housing estate now stands.

The triumphant football team of Holy Trinity Roman Catholic School, 1957/58. The team includes, standing: B. Evans, M. Murphy, S. Clarke, D. Elliott, P. McGillicuddy, T. Henry and P. Smith. Seated: A. Powney, J. Parry, J. Moore, T. Rylands and B. McMohn.

Banks Road Council School. Standard III are seen here in 1921.

Banks Road Infants class, c. 1926. The teacher, Miss Sendall, is said to have made cinder and treacle toffee to sell to the children at 1d per bag!

The Banks Road School was built in 1904, shortly after Garston became incorporated into Liverpool. Seen here is Class 1B in 1951.

St Mary's (Grassendale) Church of England School, otherwise known as Victoria High Grade School, was built in 1898 and demolished in 1990.

Pupils from Form IV, Victoria School, pictured around 1911.

Island Road Wesleyan Methodist School was opened 1897 and closed in the late 1920s, when the pupils transferred to other schools in the area. A former pupil remembered processing in pairs along Garston Old Road when she moved on to the 'Tin School' as the temporary Duncombe Road School was called. She also remembered the sandstone 'windowsills without a window' in the school yard for the children to sharpen their slate pencils on during playtime; these still today show the grooves from constant sharpening.

Island Road Wesleyan Methodist School – a performance in the school yard in 1923.

Gilmour, Southbank Road Infants School opened in 1938. Here are some of the children pictured on Empire Day in 1939.

The next generation of Gilmour, Southbank Road Infants in 1965; practical activity is now the order of the day.

A class in the late 1920s of Gilmour, Duncombe Road School which was originally built to cater for children from five years of age until they left school. However, as the population increased, new schools were built, for infants at Southbank Road and for senior boys and girls at Heath Road and Greenhill Road. The latter two eventually became part of New Heys Comprehensive School.

Jean Gay, Joan Breden, Muriel Lloyd, Ella Gartland, Lucy Dennison, Muriel Jones, Sybil Foxley, Joan Ayer, Joyce Cowley, Gladys Hastie, Edna Lovegreen, Mary Peet, Joan Watson and Joan Tewkesbury are some of the girls in Class VIII at Gilmour, Duncombe Road School in 1932.

Gilmour Boys, Secondary Modern School, Heath Road, 1947. This group includes, back row: Turner, Holt, Pearson, Parks, Thompson, Price, Hendry. Middle row: Gilks, Brewer, Mulling, Woods, Morris, Mr Smith (teacher), Thomas, Peagram, Mayers, Doorbarn. Front row: Harris, Lacey, Dane, McGregor, Hibbet, Percival.

Triumphant football team of Heath Road Boys School, 1962/63. The team included, back row: J. Barlow, L. Denton, J. Cowley, C. Carruthers and G. Godbold. Front row: L. Hunter, A. Bennett, A. Jenkins, P. Godfrey and R. Bell, with their teachers and coaches Mr A. Hutford and Mr J. Feast.

Seven

Churches and Church Life

Chapel Road. St Francis' Church parish room is on the left. This building was erected by George Heald in 1837; it was the first Methodist church in the area and stands as a memorial to his young son who, shortly before he died, aged eight, asked his father to build him a chapel. When the building became too small a new church was built a little way up the road on the corner of Island Road and Garston Old Road, opened in June 1872, (centre distance). The railway company bought the building and subsequently sold it to the Congregationalists who used it for some years until they too built a new church in Garston Old Road, near Whitehedge Road. The building was then bought by the Roman Catholics for their first place of worship. This was during the time of Father Fred Smith and it was he who rescued the old cross base from a nearby builder's yard and erected it on this site, adding to it the metal cross.

Procession in St Francis' Church grounds. Note the Baptist church in background to the left.

The young people of St Francis' Church when they presented the pantomime *Aladdin*, a short time after the Second World War.

St Austin's Roman Catholic Church. This photograph was taken before the graveyard was made smaller for the widening of the road and also before the pinnacles were removed as they were considered to be in danger of collapsing.

St Mary's Church, Grassendale. The foundation stone of the new church in Grassendale was laid by the Rector, Revd Augustus Cambell in September 1852. The church was opened in August 1853 and consecrated on 4 July 1854.

The second St Michael's Parish Church (note the third church to the right of the picture, consecrated on 29 November 1877). The 'old church' was about to be demolished and some of the stonework was subsequently used for the building of the wall surrounding the church in Church Road. The Norris family of Speke had originally funded the building of this chapel.

A concert party by the young people of the Parish Church around the turn of the century. Miss Agnes Radcliffe, well known in Garston for many years, is seen second from the right on the front row and next to her in a top hat is Arnold Clarke.

The choir of St Michael's Parish Church., taken in 1929. Seated in the centre is Revd Canon T. Parnell Rowe, MA, who was the Vicar of Garston from 1906 to 1929.

Confirmation group in the Jubilee Institute. Bishop Martin, the Bishop of Liverpool is seated in the centre and Revd E.H. Isaacs is seated to the left. He was the Vicar of Garston from 1961 to1967.

Bowden Road Presbyterian Church. The church moved to this building, which had previously been a Unitarian church, from their large building in Clifton Street and Moss Street. The Clifton Street building was then used as a baby clinic and the Moss Street entrance led to the school clinic. The building pictured above was later converted into houses.

The Bowden Road Church was very active and seen here is a Tramp Supper in 1952. Those attending were only admitted if they were suitably attired and had brought with them a jam jar in which to take their tea. The rest of their refreshments were naturally wrapped up in newspaper.

Garston Baptist Church, built in 1893. This picture shows a concert party in the early 1900s.

Here members of the Baptist Church are celebrating their Diamond Jubilee with a scrumptious tea in 1953.

Banks Road Methodist Church and school rooms were built in 1882. The church had previously, from 1871, occupied a site on the opposite side of the road on land which was bought from them by the gas works. When, in 1970, problems with dry rot caused the church building on the right to be closed, the portion of the school building to the left was converted into a chapel for worship.

Young people of Banks Road Church presenting a pantomime.

Island Road Methodist Church's Sunday School childrens' concert in 1895. This photograph was taken by Mr T.E. Lloyd who will be remembered by some as the chemist and dentist in St Marys Road. He was a keen photographer and this photograph includes two of his youngest children, Connie, (front row left) and Frank who is the little boy with his eyes closed to right of the second row.

The same Methodist Church celebrating its centenary in May 1972.

The parish of All Souls' Church began with services in the open air. The parishioners then acquired the old canteen previously used by the workers during the building of the Economic Housing Estate, sited near Garforth Road. This Hut served as their spiritual and social home for about eight years. It was fondly remembered by many people. The new church was completed in 1927 and the new parish hall in 1931.

The church grew quickly and had a large choir. The Vicar, Revd J.T. Davies (1923-1936), is seated in the centre.

Boys' Brigade District Parade 1951, in Earp Street. Garston Baptist Church Troupe are following the colours (flag) carried by Mr H.J. Evans, followed by Mr W.H. See, Company Captain. St Francis' Church can be seen in the background.

The 4th Allerton Sea Scouts in 1965. They were founded in 1916 and are seen here outside their headquarters, next to the Congregational Church, in Garston Old Road, (now the United Reformed Church), around 1970.

The 6th Allerton Scouts at their headquarters, Mulliner Field, Kettle Nook, off Woolton Road, in the early 1960s.

The 213th Liverpool Brownie Pack (St Michael's church, Garston), in October 1962, with their Brown Owl, Miss Pam Fleetwood.

Eight
War and Peace

Garston Garrison Volunteers was formed on 2 April 1860 at Garston as the 15th Corps and renumbered the 6th Corps in 1880 when it consisted entirely of position artillery. In 1908 the Corps transferred to the Territorial Force as the 3rd West Lancashire Brigade. They drilled and met in various places including the yard of the Council Offices in Garston Old Road, a building erected in a new street opposite the old National School in Kettle Nook and also in a building in Earp Street, near the corner of Seddon Road. This last headquarters was thought to have been converted from what had been used as stabling for the horses who pulled the omnibus that travelled between Garston and Liverpool, before the electric trams service started.

The War Memorial, situated on the corner of Long Lane and Woolton Road, was erected to commemorate those who lost their lives during the First World War. The railings were taken away to help the 'war effort' during the Second World War, at the end of which the lives of those who died at this time were remembered with a further inscription.

A wartime event which put Garston on the national news. On the night of 28 November 1940, during an air raid on Liverpool, a number of parachute mines fell on Garston. One landed on the gas works and hung in the gas holder without exploding. Bomb Disposal officer Lieutenant Newgass, RNVR, was assigned to make it safe. However, before he could enter the gas holder the local gas workers had already taken action to avoid an explosion and 60,000 local people were evacuated from their homes. For their courage, coolness and ability, the following awards were made: George Medal to G.N. Kermode (foreman fitter) and E. Saxon (oxy-coal gas burner); MBE to W. Morris (works manager); BEM to A.G. Kemp (fitter) and A. McRea (plumber); Commendations for Brave Conduct to H. Mason (store-keeper and first aid attendant), F. Wilson (compressor attendant) and G. Savage (fitter's labourer). Lieutenant Newgass RNVR was awarded the George Cross.

'At Home – 1940'. Seen here is land mine damage to the office block at J.J. Mills distillers. The tower seen behind supplied hydraulic power to dock machinery and has been demolished. During this or another bombing raid, Mr James H. Wheeler of Etruria Street risked his life to rescue a woman and child who were trapped, and then, although in a bad state himself, went on to help others. He was awarded the George Medal for his bravery.

'At Sea – 1940'. The crew of the *Mopan* in a prison camp in Germany. The *Mopan* was returning to Garston loaded with bananas in October 1940 when she was shelled and hit by the German battleship *Admiral Scheer*. The order was given to abandon ship and after half an hour in the water, the crew were picked up by that same battleship. After being transferred from ship to ship, always in uncomfortable conditions, they were eventually interned in a prison camp until the end of the war. Garston men who were members of that crew were, back row, extreme left, Billy Killgannon, second from left, John Donnellon, extreme right, William Taylor. Middle row, third from left, Jimmy O'Toole. Front row, fifth from left, Samuel Burnett. All eventually arrived home safely.

Bread rationing starts during the Second World War. The general manager of the Garston shops, Mr J.P. Jones (standing next to the man with the pipe) is on one of his weekly visits to Manchester. He and other managers are being given their instructions on how to proceed.

'A' Company Home Guard, based at Island Road Methodist Church. The picture includes: Jack Jones, Bert Beddon, Tom Watson, A. Harding, Joe Rawlinson, ? Shuker, W. Carter, ? Graham and two others whom we have not been able to name. An incident happened one night when a rifle went off by mistake. Fortunately the only casualty was the pinnacle of one of the railings, which with its hole right through the middle, was kept as a memento by the church.

VE Day celebrations in York Street. Note the air raid shelters in the background.

VE Day party in Russell Road; signs say 'Russell Road Children's Peace Treat' and 'God Bless the King, Mr Churchill, all our Lads and Allies'. The group includes the families of Avery, Garrett, Jones and Read.

Another Garston VE Day party in Canterbury Street. Note the air raid shelter to the right.

V J Day, September 1945. A party outside the homes of the Crowthers and Beddows families in Dingle Vale or Dale View.

Nine
Sport and Leisure

Garston has a long recorded history of its inhabitants being interested and taking part in many sporting activities: football, cycling, bowls, rifle shooting, rounders, tennis and cricket to name a few. Here we see a ladies' cricket team. The photograph was taken in 1895 by Mr T.E. Lloyd (the chemist), perhaps because his daughter Gertrude is seated on the left. The picture has the caption, 'The 1st Lady's Cricket Club. The Avenue'. They were later to share this pitch with the gentlemen players.

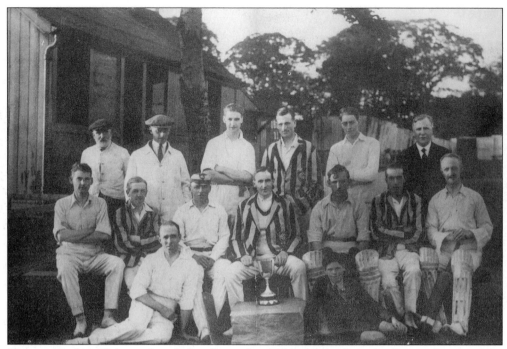

Garston Cricket Club was founded in December 1886 and the first match was played in May 1887. A tent was bought to act as a pavilion. Later, the club made its base in The Avenue.

Cartoon of Revd J.M. Swift, Vicar of Garston (1929-1945) who achieved 1,000 runs and 100 wickets in a season in 1911. The Revd J.M. Swift came to Garston in 1929. Previously he had been the Head of the Preparatory Department of the Liverpool Collage, in addition to holding the curacy of St Bridgets, Wavertree. He was a sportsman of some note and played for a number of local teams. He took a great interest in the history of Garston, as seen by the publishing of his book, *The History of Garston and its Church.*

Garston Cricket Club, this time pictured outside their 'pavilion' in 1933. The occasion was the Garston Cricket League, held at the Holly Farm Cricket Club. Many of the Garston players were well known faces at that time and are listed below:

Mr Clifton (club professional),

Alfred M. Proffitt (printing works, St Marys Road),

Mr Oakes (Garston Distillery, outdoor service),

Mr W.E. Davies (teacher, Victoria School),

Mr George Ubsdel (licensee, Palatine Hotel),

Mr Pitkethley (a fine batsman),

Mr Wilf Grimes (Gladstone Road),

Mr W. Drinkwater (Grassendale Park, insurance representative),

Malcolm McGregor (hay and provender merchant, Chapel Road and James Street),

Mr Wilson (Island Road, director of Wilson's Bobbin Works),

Mr Davey (Island Road, clerk),

Mr Woods (publican, Window Lane),

Frank Wooding (The George Hotel, St Marys Road, organiser of 'Mile of Pennies' collection for charity),

Mr Dyble (newsagent, St Marys Road, director of Lyceum Cinema and the Picturedrome, Heald Street),

Mr Leadbetter (newsagent, now McFerrans, Church Road),

George Atkin (greengrocer, Liverpool City Councillor and director of Lyceum Cinema),

Mr Pope (grocer and provision merchant, corner of Heald Street and St Marys Road),

Victor Newbold (fast demon bowler),

Alf Wilkinson (captain, dairyman, Russell Road, founder member of South Liverpool FC).

This picture was given to us complete with names; the discerning eye will notice that there are eighteen gentlemen and nineteen names! Who missed the photo shot, and what is the dog called?

The rounders team from Wilson Brothers Bobbin Works, pictured in 1918.

The Garston Cycle Club, including several members of the Crean family. Bernard and Thomas Crean are second and third from left on the back row, and young Patrick is the smallest lad on the front row.

Garston Parish Church football team with their trophies, 1916/17, with Revd Shaw. Les Gidman is seated in the centre of the middle row.

Police 'F' Division, Garston, football team.

Bessie Braddock, MP for Liverpool, presenting prizes at a bowling competition on Long Lane Recreation Ground in the 1930s.

A view of the bowling green in Banks Road. Tom Hitchen and his friends enjoy an afternoon on the green.

The Tennis Club in the 1920s. The courts were next to the Cricket Club in The Avenue. Standing on the extreme right is Robert Stopford, later Bishop of London. Also identified in the photograph are: Seymour Hunking, Tom Pritchard, John Preston, Annie Arden and Betty Southall.

A Sports and Racing Car Show in 1956. The line up here is seen outside the Autospeed Garage, opposite to the Lyceum Cinema in St Marys Road, now a supermarket and petrol station.

Garston Swimming Club in the years around 1915 was regarded as one of the best swimming clubs in the country. The swimmers won many local, national and international awards. In the 1920 Olympic Games, four women from the Garston Club represented Britain in the 4 x 100 m freestyle relay team and won a silver medal. They were: Grace McKenzie, Charlotte Radcliffe, Lillian Birkenhead (reserve) and Hilda James. Austin Rawlinson also won many awards between 1916 and 1930 and continued his connection with swimming as coach, manager and president of many swimming associations. He was the Team Manager of the British Swimming Team from 1959 to 1961, including the 1960 Olympic Games in Rome.

The 1920 British Olympic Swimming Team with the four Garston lady competitors seen centre front.

The tradition of swimming was encouraged in the local schools, particularly Banks Road, where Walter Shimmin was head teacher. He collaborated with Bill Howcroft, coach of Hilda James the Olympic competitor, to write a book *Swimming for Schoolboys*. Pictured here are the Banks Road Schoolboys Team, 1923/24.

Garston Swimming Club, 1947. Back row, from left: J. Wain, S. Boyle, E. Earp. Front row: G. Hornby, T. Crowther, R. Graham and J. Smith.

Bankfield House, the first Up the Shore race awards in 1976. About twelve young people took part. Little did they know that ten years later, there would be 1,400 entries, so the following year the event was split into two races, the Fun Run and the Devils Gallop. This latter race now attracts serious runners from all over the country. One local runner in the over 60s group thought he was doing very well when he found himself in conversation with a young man running beside him, until he discovered the said young man was just warming up for the 'big race'. Pictured with the three winners, J. Connelly (junior), J. Redmond (intermediate) and Kevin May (senior), are Mr Brian Taylor, Warden of Bankfield House, Revd T. Robinson, Dave Crumpton, the organiser, Mr Gillespy, the starter and other runners.

A later Bankfield House Fun Run. Note the Old Hangar in the background. This was built by roofing over the farmyard of Chapel House Farm, using the outbuildings as walls. The farmhouse was used as the control tower and was the beginning of Speke Airport. The hangar was, until recently demolished, the oldest surviving aircraft hangar in the country.

94

Ten
High Days and Holidays

The celebration of the coronation of King Edward VII in August 1902. The Garston Recreational Ground had been opened earlier that same year, so to celebrate the coronation, the gates of the entrance at the corner of Island Road and Clarendon Road were decorated and on the day, there were then activities for all to enjoy. Mr Joseph Rawlinson is seen here holding the reins of a horse called Bess.

Empire Day at the National School outside the Jubilee Institute. Note the stones (which will grass over), of the railway embankment. There are also spectators taking advantage of the high spots on the embankment, the roof of Grayson, Rollo and Clover, ship repair yard and even on the top of the railway signal.

The Jubilee Institute, opened in 1891, to commemorate Queen Victoria's Jubilee four years earlier. The children are with the Revd Canon T. Parnell Rowe MA. The date of the picture is not known, but Canon Rowe was the Vicar of Garston from 1906 to 1929. The photograph was taken before Caulfield's pet shop was built, (far left). The institute was demolished in 1970.

'Taking the Salute' in the 1930s beneath the Spion Cop. In the picture can be seen Canon Lindsey, Mr H.V. Davies and Mr Gilbert Knowles, church wardens, and Mr Jock Duncan the Scout Master. The scouting officer taking the salute has not been identified. A row of shops now stand on this site in Speke Road.

The crowning of the Parish Rose Queen, Edna Murray, in 1932. This celebration took place in the grounds of the Cheshire Lines Railway Social Club.

The Garston Co-operative Womens' Guild, founded in 1897. It is thought that this photograph was taken in the garden belonging to Mrs Thomas Crowther, in Hartington Road (back row on the extreme right). Mr Crowther worked for Wilson's Bobbin Works; he came from their works in Cornholme, near Todmorden, as their chief mechanic, to set up the machinery in the new works in Garston. Since the Co-operative Movement started in Rochdale, quite near to Todmorden, it could be that the wives who moved to Garston with their bobbin worker husbands were already familiar with the movement and therefore helped to strengthen this influential group in Garston.

The Garston Women's Conservative Unionist Association, another strong women's organisation, the members of which spent their time working for the betterment of Garston and its people. They are about to leave for an outing – what a wonderful vehicle to travel in!

The Garston Recreation Ground children's swing park. It is still on the same site today in Garston Old Road, but looks very different. Over the years the children have enjoyed all the different kinds of equipment provided. However, what many remember as they think of the old days, is the vigilant park keeper, whom they could, tease, fear, turn to but always respect, according to their inclination.

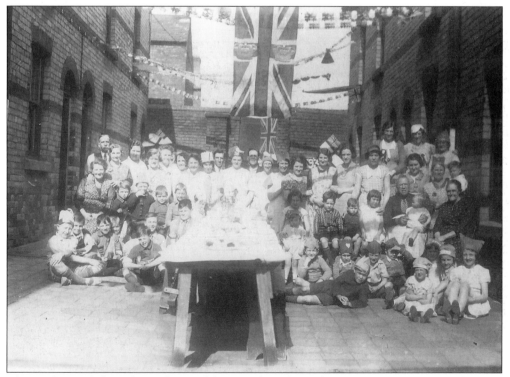

The residents of Shrewsbury Place, celebrating the Silver Jubilee of King George V and Queen Mary in June 1935.

The coronation of King George VI in May 1937 being celebrated in Byron Street.

The coronation of Queen Elizabeth II in June 1953. The celebrations in Byron Street take place outside the homes of the Davies, Parry, Webb and Ireland families.

The residents of Clifton Street celebrate the coronation of King George VI in 1937. These include the families of Atherton, Jones, Gillan, Kelly, Humphries, Kefford, Hayward, Hesketh, Walls, Boyce, McNamara, Milton, Dealey, McDaid and Thorley.

Fifteen years later in 1951. Many of those same families, to celebrate the coronation of Queen Elizabeth II, arranged an outing to Blackpool for their children, a number of whom were babes in arms in the above picture.

The coronation of King George VI in May 1937. Participating in celebrations in York Street are said to be the following as children: Mrs Fiddler, Lizzie Taylor, Mary Jones, Mrs Elliot, Mrs Robinson, Audrey Drew, Bessie and Dolly Derbyshire, Mrs Wilson, and Dolly Kitson.

The coronation party in York Street, June 1953, which included members of the families of, Stanton, McFetters, Gilmartin, Peagram, Martin, Jeavons, Tudman, Davies, Flynn, Whitehead, Langley, Simpson, Southern, Gainey, Udo, Malling, Healey, Haughton and Crumpton.

Festival of Britain, 1951. Here a celebration party is held for the residents of Speke Road Gardens.

Palmerston Road; another occasion for a party,

Mr and Mrs Joseph Rawlinson on the occasion of the opening of the Victoria Hall in Heald Street. Opened on 28 September 1907, the hall is the home of the Orange Lodge. Mr Rawlinson's firm of builders was to carry out the work. Mrs Rawlinson is seen here holding the trowel and maul, used at the Stone Laying Ceremony, a few months earlier.

Orange Lodge Procession in the 1950s, along Banks Road and Church Road. In the background can be seen Lenton's the butcher and well known Frank Ketts the pawnbrokers. Both shops were demolished in the 1960s and the site is now occupied by housing.

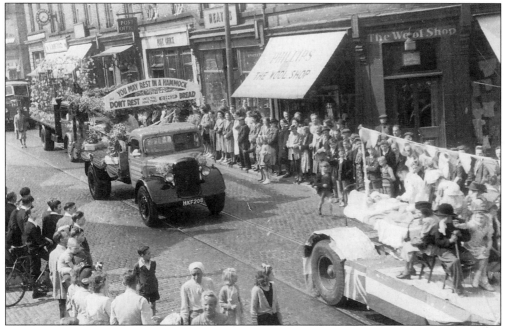

Carnival Procession in St Marys Road between Heald Street and Wellington Street. Note the post office and clock over Rimes and Co., the butchers.

The same procession between Wellington Street and James Street. Shop names can be seen on the sun blinds: Noble's, Bewley's, Chapman's and, on the right of picture, Benson's the Bed Shop. Street collectors seem to be wearing pirate costume; does this help to date it?

Carnival 1947. The Garston Girls Friendly Society entry is Sports on Parade. The group includes: P.Wood, P. Mason, B.Wain, E. Baker, A. Sutcliffe and we understand that the lady in the pill-box hat is Margaret Dovey.

Brownies from St Michael's Church in 1948. Their float is passing Speke Road Gardens.

The carnivals stopped in the 1950s. In 1975 the event was re-established and run by the Garston Community Council. It became one of the largest voluntarily run carnivals in the City of Liverpool. This picture was taken in 1975 and shows the Pandemonium Band passing Speke Road Gardens, demolished in 1983.

The Royal Order of Buffaloes outside one of their meeting places in Island Road. Their entertainment group raised a great deal of money for charity over a number of years. This photograph is said to have been taken just before their last charity outing before the Second World War. However, it is said that John J. Humphreys, the young man in sailor's uniform on the front row, came to Garston from Silloth after the war. Other known names on photograph are, F. Hayward, J. Hayward, A. Hesketh, W. Woodhouse, B. Hill, A. Pegram, C. Pegram and J. Cook.

A picnic on Grassendale Promenade in 1929. The steps were at the bottom of Beechwood Road and the Promenade is now known as Otterspool Promenade. Children include from left to right: ? Pemberton, Pauline Drew, Frank Wharton, Gwylam Pemberton, Dorothy Jones, and ? Bushell. Dorothy's mother and brother are on the steps.

The Parish Church Youth Fellowship holiday around 1940 in the Isle of Man. The group includes: Tom Brown, Graham Wyke, Stan Ball, Bill Hitchen, Audrey Houghton, Cara Lindsey, Beatie Richards, Ann Wilkinson, Alice Atherton, Stella and Marie Davies, Margaret Lawrence, Mildred Pickstock, Doris Ball, May Wood, Ruth Lindsey, Joyce Traynor, Audrey Peters, Fred Gillman and Frank Gerken among others. Canon Lindsey is seen standing on the right of the back row.

Eleven

Pubs, Shops
and Family Businesses

Garston Hotel. The above postcard, posted in 1906, shows the building before alterations to the second storey. The top room at that time was sometimes referred to as The Lighthouse or Lantern Lamp because it was used as a lookout post for ships proceeding up the Garston Channel. When a ship was spotted, a message would be sent to the Dock Offices. Note how the chimney stacks were heightened to prevent escaping smoke blocking the view from the windows. No doubt the ships also used the light from the window as a beacon. The horse drawn tanker in the road outside is thought to belong to the tar works near the docks. Note also the single track tram lines and the smart verandas of the shop on the corner of Bennett Street.

The Wellington Hotel, Wellington Street. This picture of the Wellington was taken many years ago. The Technical School, opened in 1922, has not yet been built beyond it. James Wood was the proprietor for over forty years, followed by his son. A room in it was sometimes used by the Garston Board for its meetings, before Garston was incorporated into Liverpool, in 1902.

Blackburne Arms, King Street, formerly the Cock and Trumpet after the device on the coat of arms of the Blackburne family (seen on the window above the door), once owners of the Manor of Garston. Members of the Tushingham family ran this concern for many years and, more recently, Greenalls Brewery have tried unsuccessfully to re-establish its use. It now stands in a sadly dilapidated state

The Queens Hotel (still standing today) and the Mona Castle, (demolished 1982), on opposite corners at the junction of St Marys Road and Church Road. In 1922 the licensee of the Mona (below) was John McKenzie and some years later it was Sarah McKenzie. Edith, their daughter, became Mrs Thompson and, with her husband, became the licensees of the Queens Hotel (above). The Mona Castle had to be demolished in 1984 for structural reasons because the back of the building had been built on rock (where once stood Garston Hall) and the front on what had been the bed of the river. The Garston and District Historical Society was offered the building as a Heritage Centre, for a peppercorn rent of £1 a year, but unfortunately could not raise the £60,000 needed to make the building structurally safe.

Volunteer Arms, Chapel Road. This former pub closed in the 1920s. The name may be connected to the formation of a volunteer militia in the nineteenth century when England felt threatened by the rise of Emperor Napoleon III in France.

Home Guard Club, Woolton Road. The occupant was recorded in 1841 as a beer-seller, and this use continued until 1922 with various proprietors. Believed at one time to have been called the Liverpool Arms, it then became the Market Members Club, then the Woolton Road Social Club and finally, in 1946, the Home Guard Club, which has replaced the building with a more modern one.

An outing setting off from the Palatine Hotel, Woolton Road.

The Stanley Arms in St Marys Road. Although it existed before 1889, the licensee at that time is recorded as J. Rawlinson, followed by a number of others until 1921. The building was then used for other purposes. In more recent years the building collapsed, was replaced and has now been converted into flats. This site is next to the present Garston Garden Centre.

The King's Vaults Public House. It is also known as McGarry's after the well known proprietor Mrs McGarry. She took over when her husband died and on her death, the establishment continued to be run by members of the McGarry family for some years.

Right: The Clarence Hotel, on the corner of York Street and Window Lane. This public house was run by the Wood Family in the 1880s. In late 1903 the proprietor became Mr Thomas Tushingham who was followed by his son in 1922. It was demolished in 1984. Left: The Cressington Hotel in 1953, situated on the corner of Eslington Street and St Marys Road. One of its proprietors from 1925 was called The Admiral because he had been given the names Raleigh, Frobisher and Drake at his baptism. The building was demolished in the 1960s to accommodate the road widening.

John Case, butcher. This was a long established butchers shop on the corner of Russell Road and Shrewsbury Road. John Case became a City Councillor, later an Alderman, and played an important part in the development of Garston. His son Roland also became a local butcher.

Ridyard's grocery store on the corner of James Street and St Marys Road.

Station Garage, Woolton Road, opposite Garston Station. The house was originally called Ashlands. The garage has been worked by Rutter's, Johnson's, Hyland's and Mansfield's.

Ingham's cobblers shop, viewed from Church Road, looking towards the hospital. Many years ago this was the Ring O' Bells public house.

Garston Co-operative Society, St Marys Road branch. Chrissy Rutter, a member of the Rutter family who owned the Station Garage, is seen third from right.

Staff at the Long Lane branch of the Co-op, taken about 1938. Seated in the centre is the manager, Mr John P. Jones who later became general manager of all the Co-op shops in the area and worked from the office in St Marys Road. Also featured are, Wilf George, Reg Exley, Ted Minnett, Alf Purcell, Ian Nickleson and a lady identified only as Peggy.

Helsbys, St Marys Road. A confectioners and, according to the notice in the first floor window, also a luncheon room. Advertisements in the shop window tempt you to teas, chops and steaks.

Bernard Crean, coal merchant. Mr Crean is seen here with his men and wagon, around 1900. The Crean family were active members of the newly formed St Francis' Church.

Window Lane. The lady in the apron is Mrs Hudson outside her sweet and meat shop. She was well known for her '1d Hot Pot Dinners'.

'Stop Me And Buy One'. Mr Smith the ice cream seller in Chesterton Street. Did the children peeping out from behind listen out for his bell?

Garston Market. This poem was given to us by Tom Giblin, who for over thirty years had a
carpet and furniture stall in the 'back shed'; many will remember him. He told us how one very
rainy day when there were few customers, 'Harold from the shoe stall' picked up a piece of shoe
box cardboard from the floor and wrote this poem. He later threw it back onto the floor, from
where Tom rescued it and kept it as a memento of his Garston Market days.

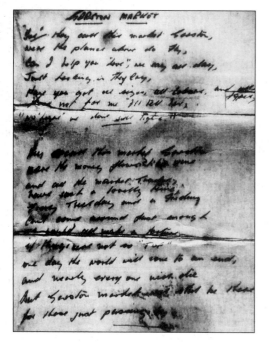

A Market Trader's Lament

Yes, they call this market Garston,
Where the planes above do fly.
'Can I help you love?' we say all day,
'Just looking' they reply.
They ask for all sizes, all colours and all types,
'They're not for me'. I'll tell her
'No love we don't sell tights'.
They call this market Garston,
Where the money flows like wine,
And all the market traders
Have such a lovely time.
We would all make a fortune
If things were not so 'tuff'.
One day the world will end,
And nearly all will die.
But, Garston Market will still be there
For those 'Just Passing By'.

120

Twelve
Street Scenes

Workers completing the pavements after tree planting in Bowden Road. In the background, left, can be seen No.1a Calthorpe Street and to the right the Unitarian, later Presbyterian, Chapel. In the middle distance are houses in Lumley Street.

St Marys Road looking south. On the right, note the cycle shop with a bicycle above the doorway. This is on the corner of Woodger Street and later became Appleton's hardware shop. The Old Cottage can just be seen at the bottom of the village.

St Marys Road looking south. Moss Street is on the left, the sign on the right of the first shop says 'Garston Post Office'. On the right hand side of St Marys Road was the Theatre Royal, the sign for which is just visible.

St Marys Road looking north. The Midland Bank building is on the right.

St Marys Road looking north. This postcard is reminiscent of a Lowry painting. Mona Street is on the left and Lloyd's the chemist is the taller building on the right.

Dock Road. The railway station closed because of lack of use once the electric tram service started. This was rather ironic as the trams' predecessor, the horse-drawn omnibus from Garston to Liverpool, ceased when the railway provided a quicker service. In 1984 the level crossing gates and the track were removed with the arrival of the by-pass.

Woolton Road, around 1900. Horse drawn carts and hand carts ply the streets. The houses on the extreme right have now been replaced by a newer complex.

Window Lane. The post office is on the right, however, most people seem to remember it being on the other side of the road!

Church Road photographed from King Street. A good view of the Parish Church, with the incinerator chimney in the background. To the left of the Blackburne Arms is the store of James Nelson and Sons Ltd. On the right would appear to be Champions and a hairdressing salon. Frank Ketts' pawnbrokers shop is, probably, just off the picture.

Clarendon Road. The first two houses to be built in this road were between Hartington Road and Long Lane and were lived in by Mr R.W. Jones JP and Mr S. Roberts. These gentlemen were proud to be the first two people to buy tickets (first class) to travel to Liverpool on the new railway. Many successful people have lived in the few houses in the picture: Robert Stopford, later a Bishop of London, was born in the first one on the left. A governor of Newfoundland, principals and professors of universities, top tycoons in both the USA and this country, reverend gentlemen and a distinguished portrait painter who has painted both the Queen and the Duke of Edinburgh as well as a number of other, locally well-known, people have all called these houses 'home'.

Woolton Road in 1926. This is the bridge over the railway before Horrocks Avenue was built. The old Station House can clearly be seen on the right and on the left is Ashlands, later to become a garage and petrol station.

Granville Road. One of Mason's cows heads back from the fields to the shippen just off the picture to the right. The Garston Cross is on its second site, before being moved to the grounds of St Francis' church.

Argyle Road in the early 1900s. Note the cobbled roadway and the very tall telegraph pole. The shop may have been a provisions and flour dealer.

A last page reminder of past glories: the Stalbridge Dock looking towards the chimneys of the industrial estate which brought wealth and prosperity to the town in the late 1800s and early 1900s.

The last remnants of the old village about to disappear, as Mr Joseph Rawlinson and his men prepare to demolish the Old Cottage. The site is now occupied by the Leading Light (see explanation elsewhere in this book). In the background are the newer developments of St Marys Road. Apart from the Queens Hotel, these shops were to give way to a supermarket and car park within less than sixty years. Garston stands poised to enter a new era of development and change, perhaps we should make greater efforts to record the 'now' for future generations.